Mel Bay's Modern
GUITAR METHOD GRADE 1

Mel Bay's Modern Guitar Method is the world's premier guitar course of instruction. Grade 1 presents basic material necessary to play contemporary guitar. Includes music theory, technical etudes and studies, solos, duets, and chord studies in the keys of C, A minor, G, and E minor.

Online Audio & Video

Audio
www.melbay.com/93200EB
Video
dv.melbay.com/93200
You Tube
www.melbay.com/93200V

Audio Contents

1	*Tuning the Guitar*
	• Notes on the E String •
2	*1st String Etude*
3	*Etude #2*
4	*The Mixmaster*
	• Notes on the B String •
5	*The Merry Men*
6	*Frolic*
7	*E-B*
	• Notes on the G String •
8	*Sparkling Stella*
9	*Aura Lee*
10	*Red River Valley*
11	*Psalm 100*
12	*When the Saints Go Marchin' In*
	• Notes on the D String •
13	*Cockles and Mussels*
14	*Eighth-Note Studies #1-6*
15	*Amazing Grace*
16	*Tenting Tonight*
17	*Melancholy*
	• Notes on the A String •
18	*Buffalo Gals*
19	*Chester*
20	*Kum-Ba-Ya*
21	*Michael, Row the Boat Ashore*
	• Notes on the Low E String •
22	*Minor Melody*
23	*Hitting on All Six*
24	*First Duet*
25	*The Repeater/Duet*
26	*The Chord Waltz*
27	*The Builder*
28	*Follow the Leader/Duet*
29	*Bass Solos with Chord Accompaniment*
30	*Gliding Along*
	• The Key of C •
31	*Shenandoah*

32	*The Blue Bells of Scotland*
33	*Long, Long Ago*
34	*A Daily Scale Study*
35	*Running Around*
36	*Home, Home, Can I Forget Thee?*
37	*Playtime/Duet*
	• The Key of A Minor •
38	*A Daily Scale Study*
39	*Wayfarin' Stranger*
40	*Cradle Song*
41	*Billy's Duet*
42	*Another Daily Scale Study in A Minor*
43	*A Visit to the Relatives*
44	*Careless Love*
45	*Song Without Words/Duet*
46	*Terry's Tune*
	• The Key of G •
47	*In the Evening by the Moonlight*
48	*Etude/Duet*
49	*The Old Mill/Duet*
50	*A Serenade*
51	*Austrian Hymn/Duet*
52	*Home on the Range*
53	*The Little Prince/Duet*
54	*Carry Me Back to Old Virginny*
	• The Key of E Minor •
55	*E Minor Scales/Harmonic, Melodic*
56	*Morning Song*
57	*Cindy*
58	*Night Song*
59	*Lament*
60	*Maytime/Duet*
61	*Rondo/Duet*
62	*Sor's Waltz*
63	*Bluegrass Waltz*
64	*Running the 3rds in G*
65	*A Little Bit of Hanon*
66	*Southern Fried*

Visit us on the Web at www.melbay.com — E-mail us at email@melbay.com

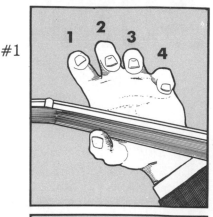

#1

#2

Place your fingers FIRMLY on the strings DIRECTLY BEHIND THE FRETS.

The correct way to hold the guitar.

#1

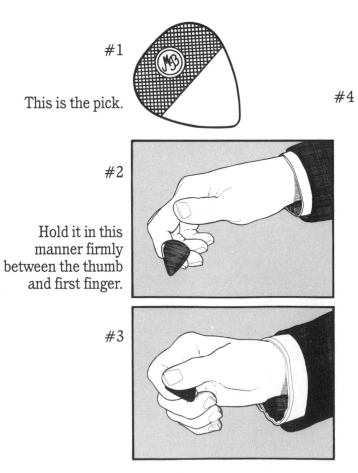

This is the pick.

#2

Hold it in this manner firmly between the thumb and first finger.

#3

⊓ = DOWN STROKE OF THE PICK.

#4

Tuning the Guitar

The six open strings of the guitar will be of the same pitch as the six notes shown in the illustration of the piano keyboard. Note that five of the strings are below the middle C of the piano keyboard.

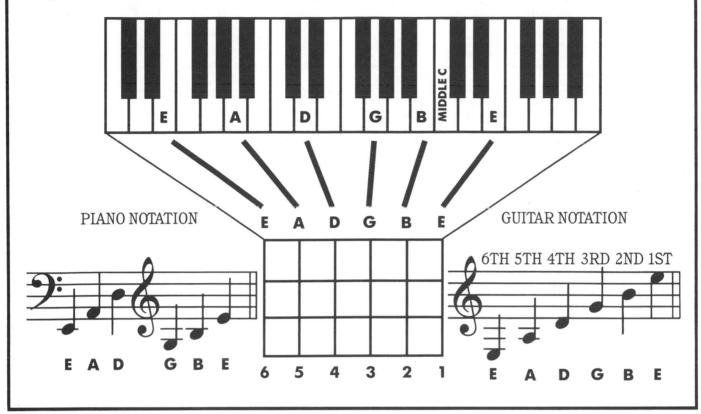

PIANO NOTATION

GUITAR NOTATION

Another Method of Tuning

1. Tune the 6th string in unison with the **E** or 12th white key to the LEFT of MIDDLE C on the piano.

2. Place the finger behind the fifth fret of the 6th string. This will give you the tone or pitch of the 5th string **(A).**

3. Place finger behind the fifth fret of the 5th string to get the pitch of the 4th string **(D).**

4. Repeat same procedure to obtain the pitch of the 3rd string **(G).**

5. Place finger behind the fourth fret of the 3rd string to get the pitch of the 2nd string **(B).**

6. Place finger behind the fifth fret of the 2nd string to get the pitch of the 1st string **(E).**

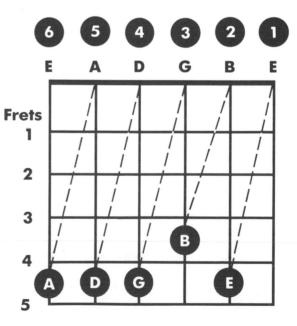

Electronic Guitar Tuner

Electronic Guitar Tuners are available at your music store. They are a handy device and highly recommended.

3

THE STAFF:

Music is written on a STAFF consisting of FIVE LINES and FOUR SPACES. The lines and spaces are numbered upward as shown:

5TH LINE ————————————————————————————
            4TH SPACE
4TH LINE ————————————————————————————
            3RD SPACE
3RD LINE ————————————————————————————
            2ND SPACE
2ND LINE ————————————————————————————
            1ST SPACE
1ST LINE ————————————————————————————

The lines and spaces are named after letters of the alphabet.

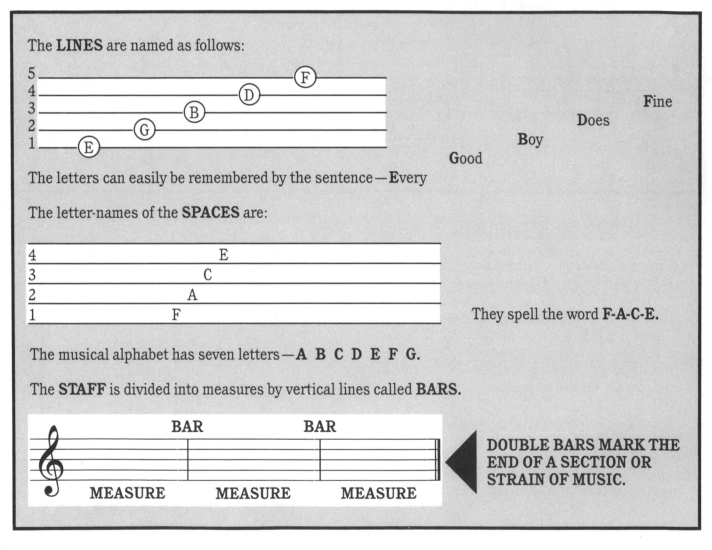

The **LINES** are named as follows:

The letters can easily be remembered by the sentence—**Every Good Boy Does Fine**

The letter-names of the **SPACES** are:

They spell the word **F-A-C-E.**

The musical alphabet has seven letters—**A B C D E F G.**

The **STAFF** is divided into measures by vertical lines called **BARS.**

DOUBLE BARS MARK THE END OF A SECTION OR STRAIN OF MUSIC.

THE CLEF:

This sign is the treble or G clef.

All guitar music will be written in this clef.

The second line of the treble clef is known as the G line. Many people call the treble clef the G clef because it circles around the G line.

NOTES

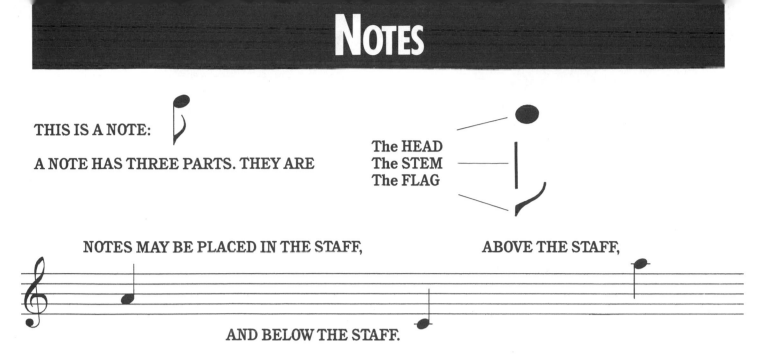

THIS IS A NOTE:

A NOTE HAS THREE PARTS. THEY ARE

The HEAD
The STEM
The FLAG

NOTES MAY BE PLACED IN THE STAFF,

ABOVE THE STAFF,

AND BELOW THE STAFF.

A note will bear the name of the line or space it occupies on the staff.
The location of a note in, above, or below the staff will indicate the pitch.

PITCH: the height or depth of a tone.
TONE: a musical sound.

TYPES OF NOTES

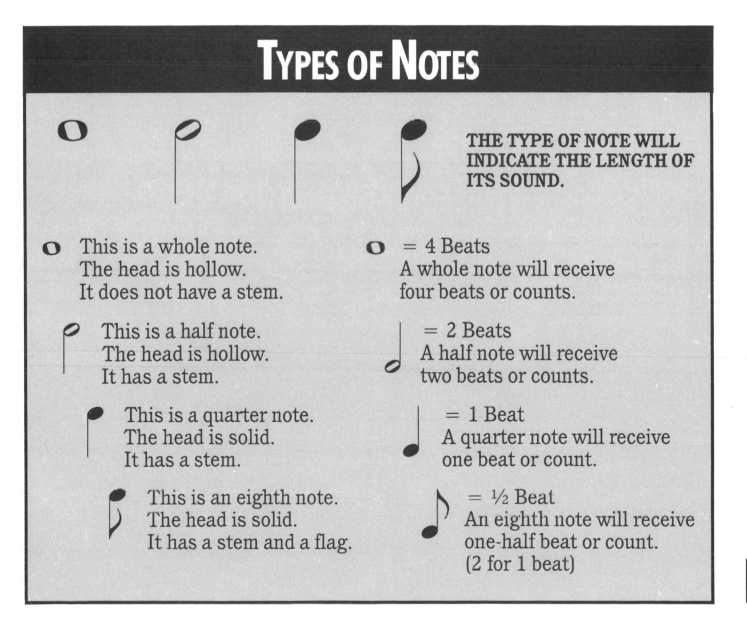

THE TYPE OF NOTE WILL INDICATE THE LENGTH OF ITS SOUND.

This is a whole note.
The head is hollow.
It does not have a stem.

= 4 Beats
A whole note will receive four beats or counts.

This is a half note.
The head is hollow.
It has a stem.

= 2 Beats
A half note will receive two beats or counts.

This is a quarter note.
The head is solid.
It has a stem.

= 1 Beat
A quarter note will receive one beat or count.

This is an eighth note.
The head is solid.
It has a stem and a flag.

= ½ Beat
An eighth note will receive one-half beat or count.
(2 for 1 beat)

RESTS

A REST is a sign used to designate a period of silence. This period of silence will be of the same duration of time as the note to which it corresponds.

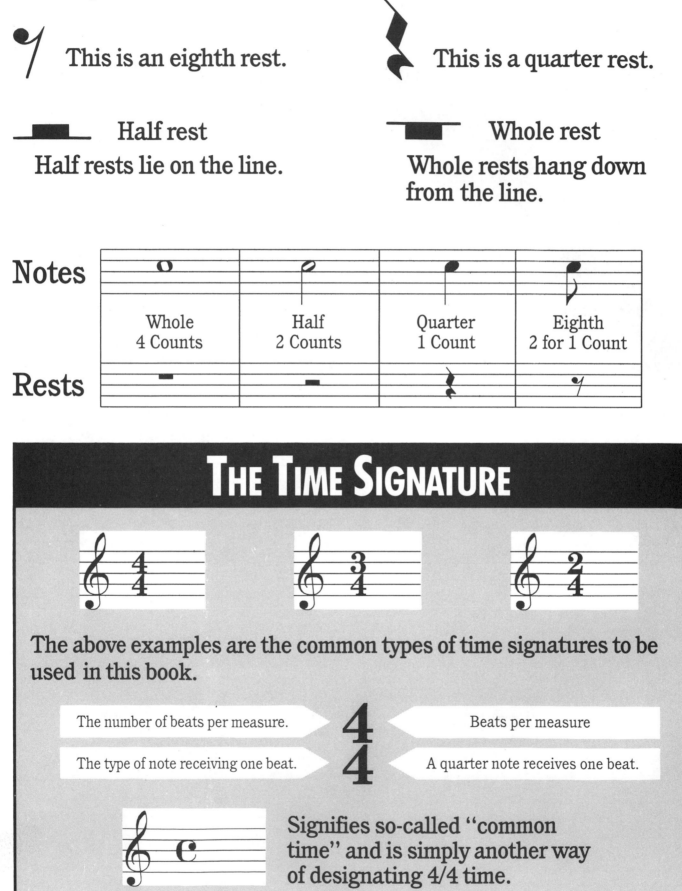

This is an eighth rest.

This is a quarter rest.

Half rest
Half rests lie on the line.

Whole rest
Whole rests hang down from the line.

Notes				
	Whole 4 Counts	Half 2 Counts	Quarter 1 Count	Eighth 2 for 1 Count
Rests				

THE TIME SIGNATURE

The above examples are the common types of time signatures to be used in this book.

The number of beats per measure.

$\frac{4}{4}$

Beats per measure

The type of note receiving one beat.

A quarter note receives one beat.

Signifies so-called "common time" and is simply another way of designating 4/4 time.

(FIRST STRING)

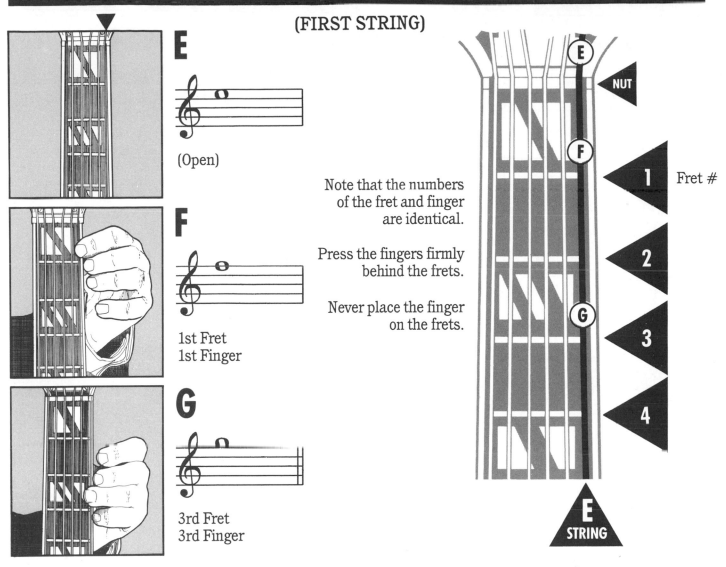

E

(Open)

F

1st Fret
1st Finger

G

3rd Fret
3rd Finger

Note that the numbers
of the fret and finger
are identical.

Press the fingers firmly
behind the frets.

Never place the finger
on the frets.

WHOLE Notes(○) receive four beats.

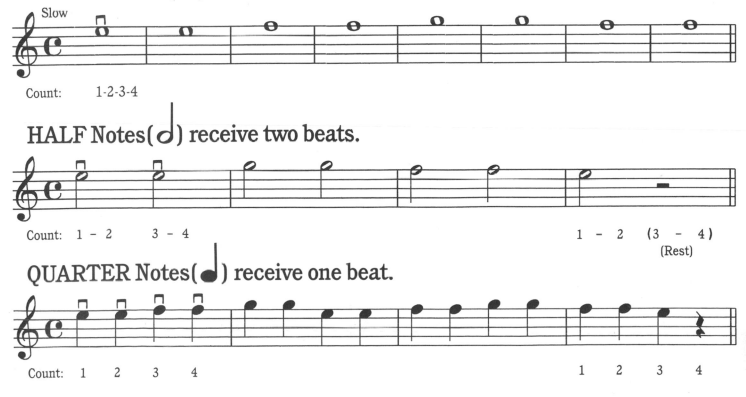

Count: 1-2-3-4

HALF Notes(♩) receive two beats.

Count: 1 − 2   3 − 4   1 − 2 (3 − 4)
                                                                              (Rest)

QUARTER Notes(♩) receive one beat.

Count: 1   2   3   4   1   2   3   4

7

1st-String Etude

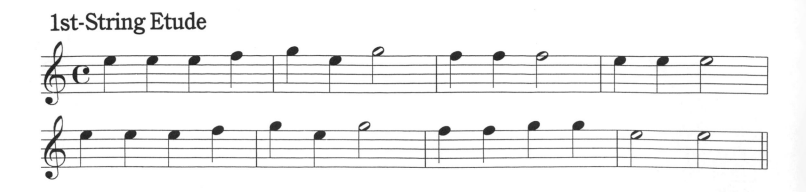

Etude No. 2

The Mixmaster

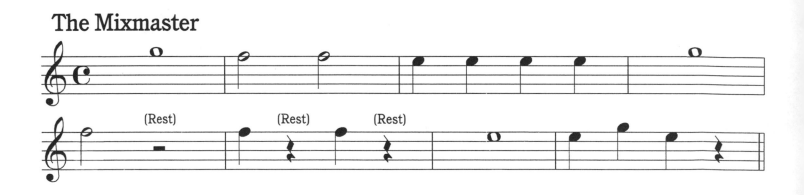

NOTES ON THE FIRST STRING

(Fill in the Blocks)

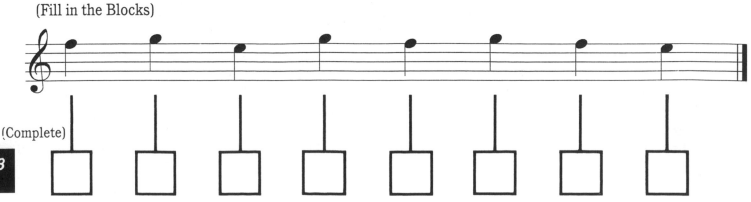

(Complete)

NOTES ON THE B STRING

(SECOND STRING)

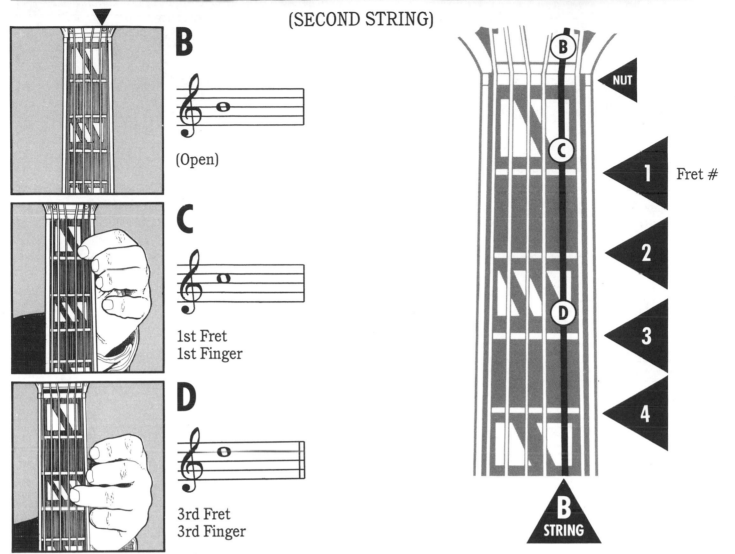

B

(Open)

C

1st Fret
1st Finger

D

3rd Fret
3rd Finger

WHOLE NOTES

Count: 1 - 2   3 - 4

HALF NOTES

Count: 1-2   3   4

QUARTER NOTES

Count: 1   2   3   4

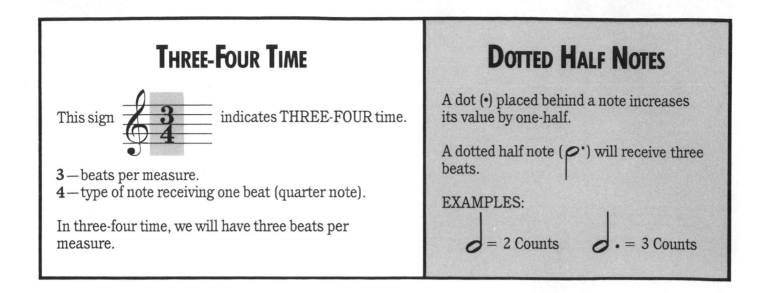

THREE-FOUR TIME

This sign **3/4** indicates THREE-FOUR time.

3 — beats per measure.
4 — type of note receiving one beat (quarter note).

In three-four time, we will have three beats per measure.

DOTTED HALF NOTES

A dot (•) placed behind a note increases its value by one-half.

A dotted half note (♩•) will receive three beats.

EXAMPLES:

♩ = 2 Counts   ♩• = 3 Counts

The Merry Men

Frolic

E—B

(THIRD STRING)

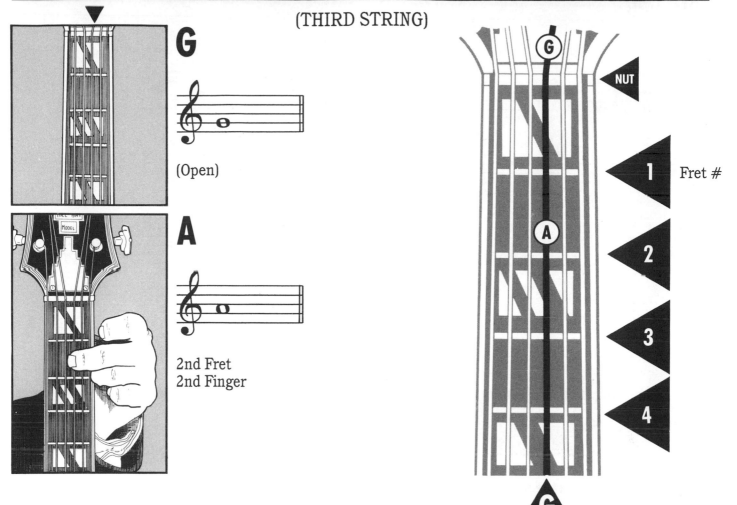

G (Open)

A 2nd Fret 2nd Finger

Fret #

NUT

1

2

3

4

G STRING

A Study on the Third String

Count: 1- 2- 3- 4

Sparkling Stella

11

Aura Lee

Folk Song

PICK-UP NOTES

One or more notes at the beginning of a strain before the first measure are referred to as "pick-up notes."

The rhythm for pick-up notes is taken from the last measure of the selection and the beats are counted as such.

Red River Valley

Teacher Acc.

Western Song

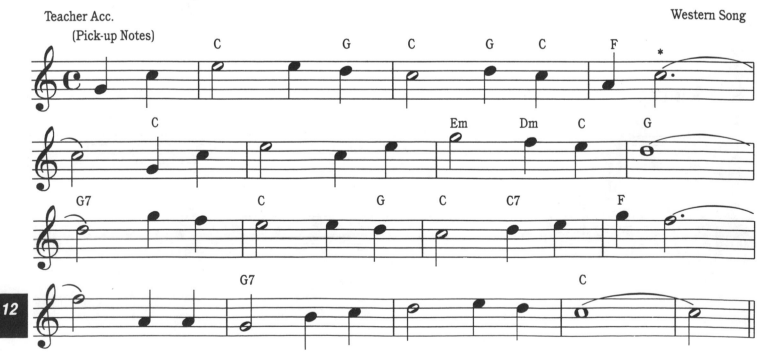

*See "The Tie" on the top of page 13.

THE TIE

The TIE is a curved line between two notes of the same pitch. The first note is played and held for the time duration of both. The second note is not played, but held.

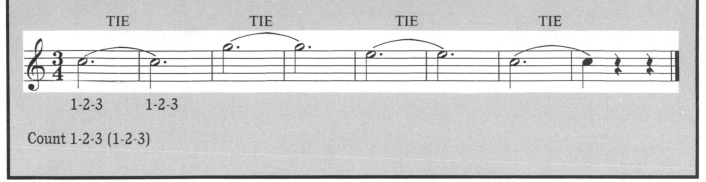

Count 1-2-3 (1-2-3)

Psalm 100

Teacher Acc.

Louis Bourgeois
1510—1561

When the Saints go Marchin' In

Teacher Acc.

Spiritual

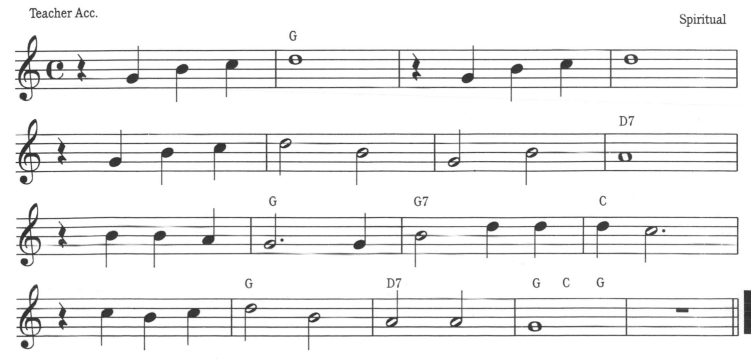

NOTES ON THE D STRING

(FOURTH STRING)

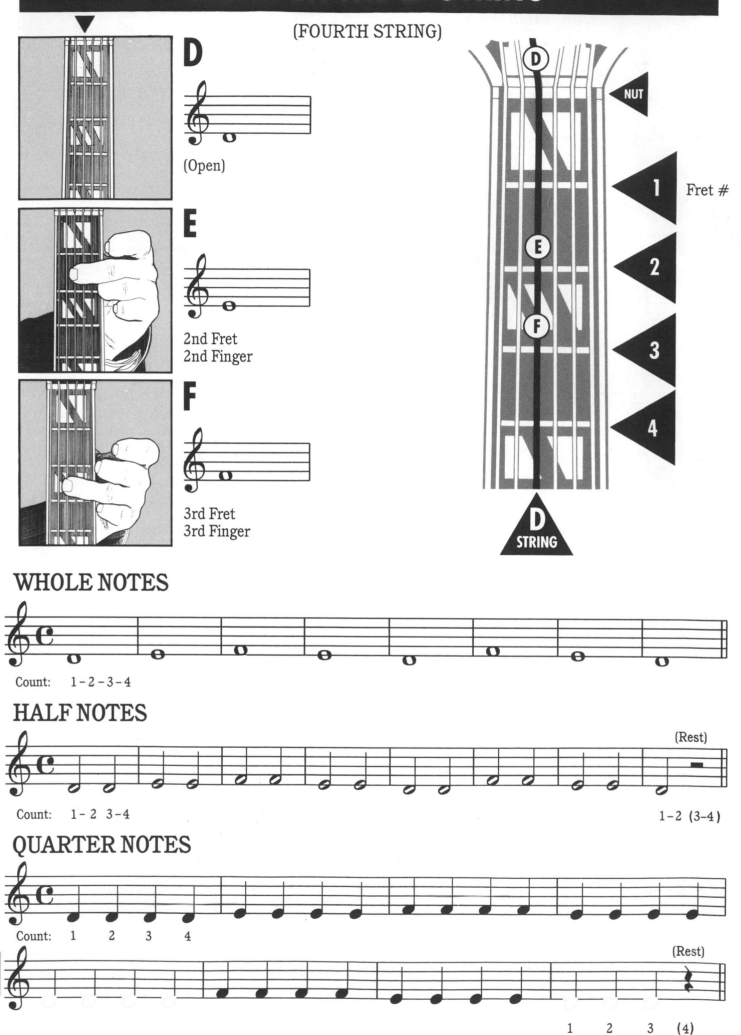

D (Open)

E 2nd Fret 2nd Finger

F 3rd Fret 3rd Finger

Fret #

NUT

D STRING

WHOLE NOTES

Count: 1 – 2 – 3 – 4

HALF NOTES

Count: 1 – 2   3 – 4

(Rest)

1 – 2 (3 – 4)

QUARTER NOTES

Count: 1   2   3   4

(Rest)

1   2   3   (4)

Cockles and Mussels

Ballad

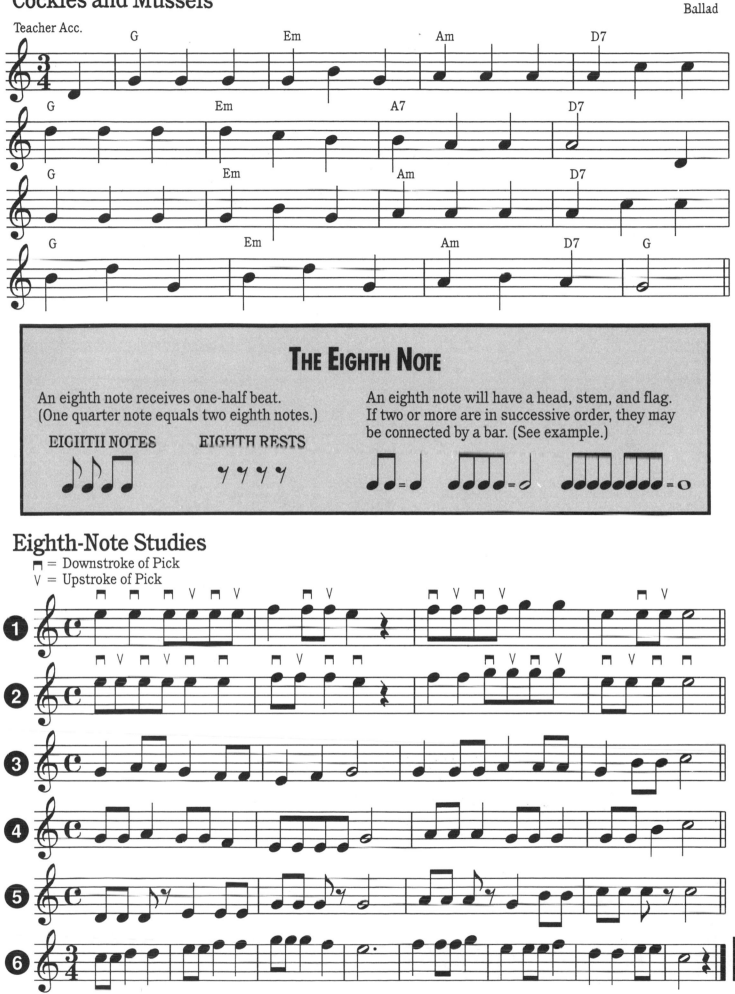

THE EIGHTH NOTE

An eighth note receives one-half beat. (One quarter note equals two eighth notes.)

EIGHTH NOTES

EIGHTH RESTS

An eighth note will have a head, stem, and flag. If two or more are in successive order, they may be connected by a bar. (See example.)

Eighth-Note Studies

⊓ = Downstroke of Pick
V = Upstroke of Pick

Amazing Grace

Hymn

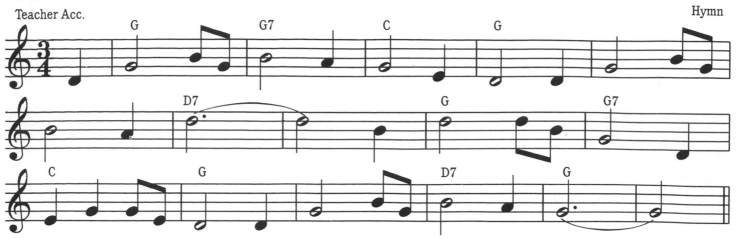

Tenting Tonight

Song of the Civil War

Melancholy

W. Bay

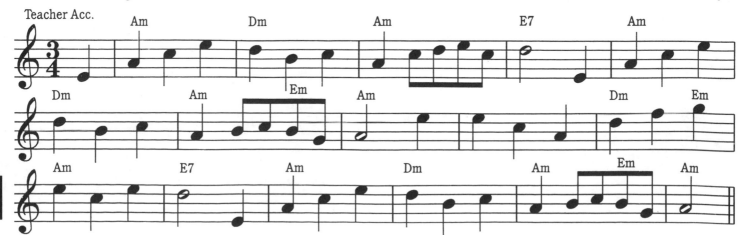

16

LEDGER LINES

When the pitch of a musical sound is below or above the staff, the notes are then placed on or between extra lines called LEDGER LINES.

They will be like this:

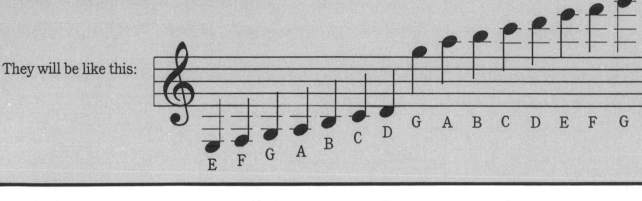

NOTES ON THE A STRING

(FIFTH STRING)

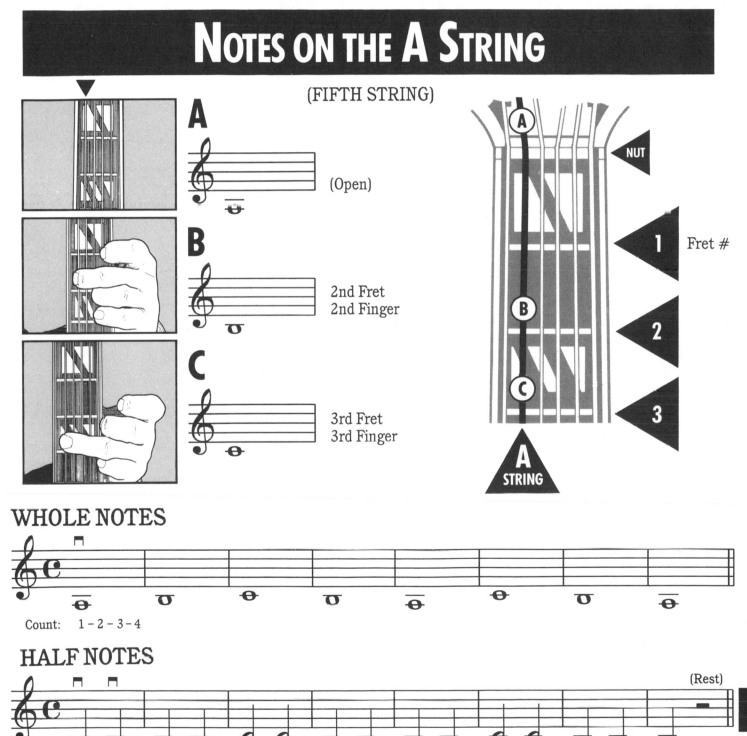

A (Open)

B 2nd Fret
2nd Finger

C 3rd Fret
3rd Finger

WHOLE NOTES

Count: 1 – 2 – 3 – 4

HALF NOTES

(Rest)

Count: 1 – 2   3 – 4

QUARTER NOTES

Buffalo Gals

Western Song

Chester

Teacher Acc.

Song of the Revolutionary War

18

DOTTED QUARTER NOTES

A DOT after a note increases its value by one-half.

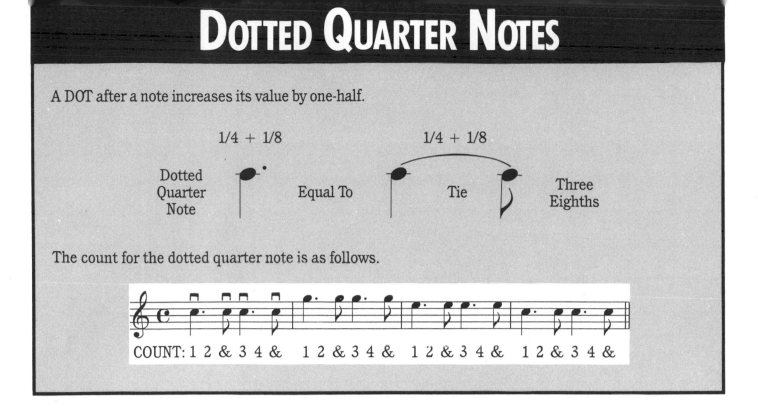

$$1/4 + 1/8 \qquad\qquad 1/4 + 1/8$$

Dotted Quarter Note Equal To Tie Three Eighths

The count for the dotted quarter note is as follows.

COUNT: 1 2 & 3 4 &   1 2 & 3 4 &   1 2 & 3 4 &   1 2 & 3 4 &

Kum-Ba-Ya

Teacher Acc.

African Hymn

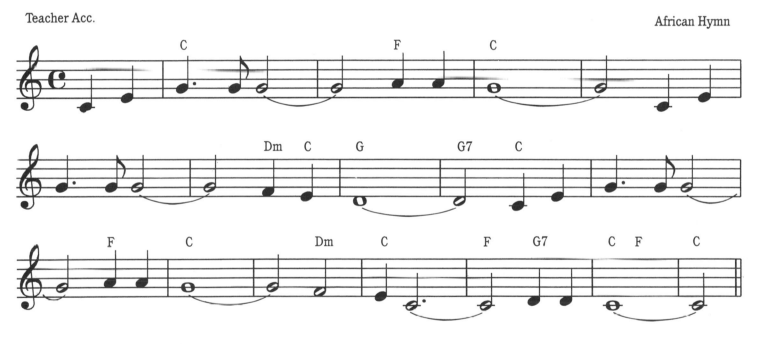

Michael, Row the Boat Ashore

Teacher Acc.

Spiritual

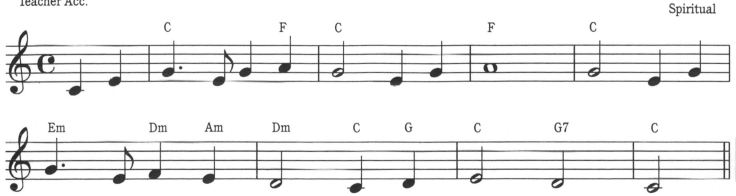

NOTES ON THE E STRING

(SIXTH STRING)

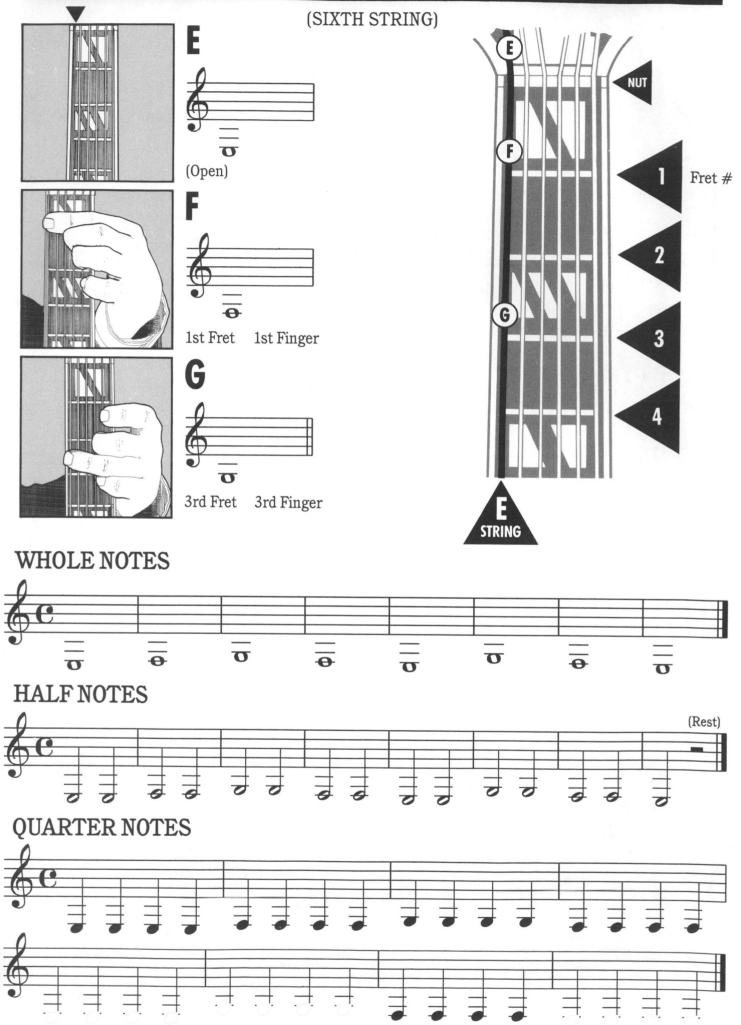

E

(Open)

F

1st Fret   1st Finger

G

3rd Fret   3rd Finger

WHOLE NOTES

HALF NOTES

(Rest)

QUARTER NOTES

INTRODUCING THE A NOTE

A

5th Fret
4th Finger

E
STRING

Minor Melody

Teacher Acc.

W. Bay

Am   Dm   E7   Am
Dm   E7   Am   G   E7   Am
Dm   Am   C   G   Am   E7   Am

NOTES ON THE GUITAR IN THE FIRST POSITION

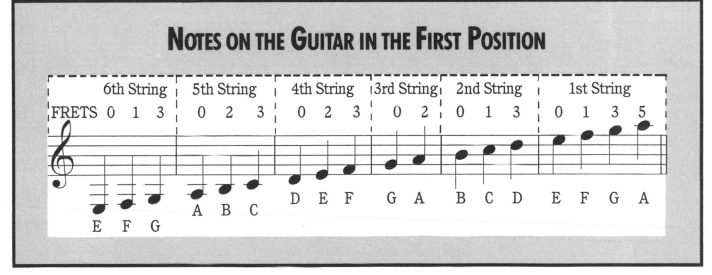

	6th String	5th String	4th String	3rd String	2nd String	1st String
FRETS	0 1 3	0 2 3	0 2 3	0 2	0 1 3	0 1 3 5

E F G   A B C   D E F   G A   B C D   E F G A

Hitting on All Six

Mel Bay

A WORD ABOUT DUETS

One of the first requisites of a good guitarist is the ability to play well with others. It is with this point in mind that I am stressing the value of duet training.

The modern guitarist has to have the ability to play SOLO, HARMONY, and RHYTHM.

Duet training will teach the student to perform his or her own part independently without the bewilderment or confusion caused by the rhythm or counterpoint appearing in the second part.

This is one of the most important phases of the student's training.

The second part in the following duets will be played by the teacher. The student will be required to play both parts later.

Our First Duet

Arr. by Mel Bay

Guitar Duet

Dots before and after a double bar mean repeat the measures between.

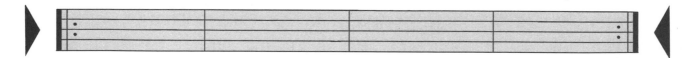

The Repeater

I = 1st Part
II = 2nd Part

The dots placed above and below the third line of the staff at the double bar indicate that the piece is to be repeated.

CHORDS

A MELODY is a succession of single tones.

A CHORD is a combination of tones sounded together.

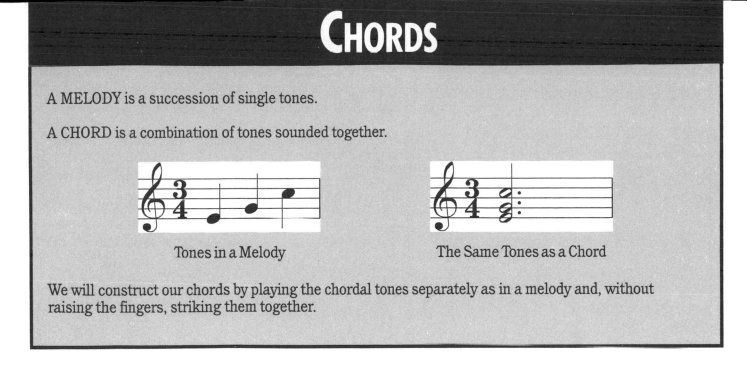

Tones in a Melody   The Same Tones as a Chord

We will construct our chords by playing the chordal tones separately as in a melody and, without raising the fingers, striking them together.

The Chord Waltz
Mel Bay

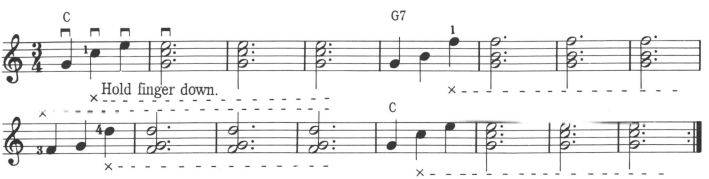

Hold finger down.

The Builder
Mel Bay

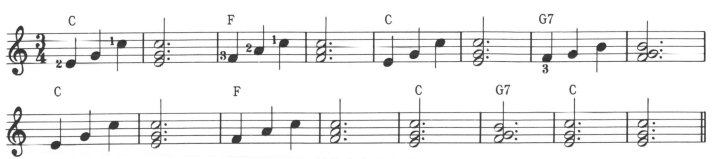

Small Chord Etude
Mel Bay

Practice the above etude until it can be played without missing a beat.

*Note that the first finger holds down two notes (C-F) in the second chord.

23

FOUR-STRING CHORD STUDY

We use the same method for building four-string chords as we did in building the three-string chords. Play the chordal tones melodically, holding the fingers down until chord is reached, then strike them together producing the desired chord.

EXERCISE

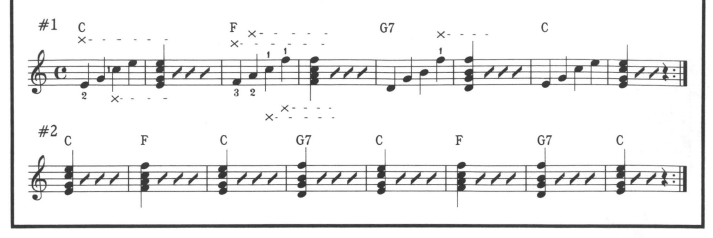

Follow the Leader

Arr. by Mel Bay

Guitar Duet

BASS SOLOS WITH CHORD ACCOMPANIMENT

When playing bass solos with chord accompaniment, you will find the solo with the stems turned downward and the accompaniment with the stems turned upward.

COUNT: 1   2   3

In the example shown above, you see the dotted half note (E) with the stem downward. It is played on the count of one and is held for counts two and three.

The quarter rest over the dotted half note indicates that there is no chord accompaniment at the count of one. The chords with the stems upward are played on counts of two and three.

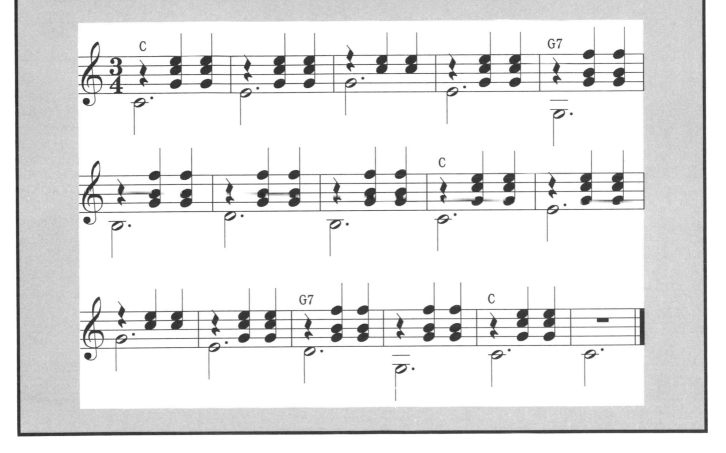

Gliding Along

Mel Bay

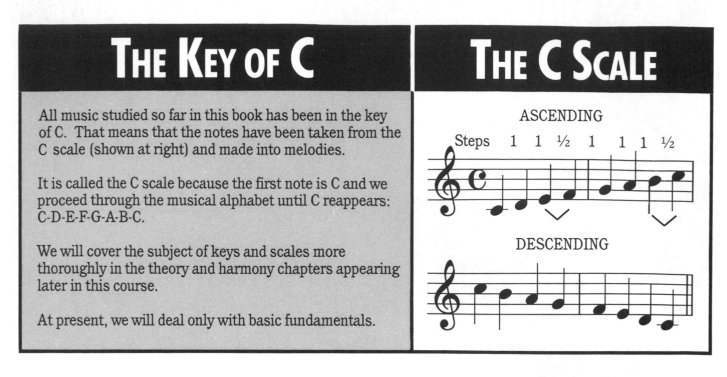

THE KEY OF C

All music studied so far in this book has been in the key of C. That means that the notes have been taken from the C scale (shown at right) and made into melodies.

It is called the C scale because the first note is C and we proceed through the musical alphabet until C reappears: C-D-E-F-G-A-B-C.

We will cover the subject of keys and scales more thoroughly in the theory and harmony chapters appearing later in this course.

At present, we will deal only with basic fundamentals.

THE C SCALE

ASCENDING

Steps 1 1 ½ 1 1 1 ½

DESCENDING

If the following arrangement on "Shenandoah" is difficult for the student at this point, the arrangement may be simplified by playing only the top two notes of each chord. A good way to learn this solo is to begin by playing only the top note of each chord and then gradually adding other notes as the student progresses.

Shenandoah

Arr. by W. Bay

The Blue Bells of Scotland

Arr. by Mel Bay

Guitar Solo

CHORDS IN THE KEY OF C MAJOR

The key of C has three principle chords. They are C, F, and G7.

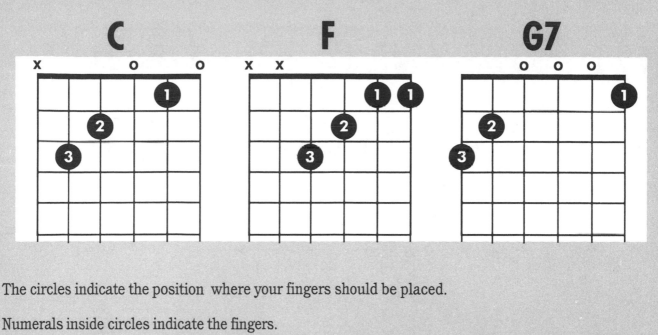

The circles indicate the position where your fingers should be placed.

Numerals inside circles indicate the fingers.

"X" over the strings means that the strings are not to be played.

"O" over the strings indicates the strings to be played open.

Place fingers in positions indicated by the circles and strike them all together.

MUSICAL NOTATION OF THE CHORDS

ACCOMPANIMENT STYLES

ALTERNATE BASSES

In Three-Four Time

Long, Long Ago

Arr. by Mel Bay

Guitar Solo

Andante

A Daily Scale Study

Mel Bay

Count: 1 & 2 & 3 & 4 &

(Repeat ⊓V⊓V)

The above study should be played slowly with a gradual increase of speed until a moderate tempo has been reached. It is an excellent daily exercise.

CHROMATICS

The alteration of the pitches of tones is brought about by the use of symbols called CHROMATICS (also referred to as ACCIDENTALS).

THE SHARP # The sharp placed before a note raises its pitch ½ step or one fret.

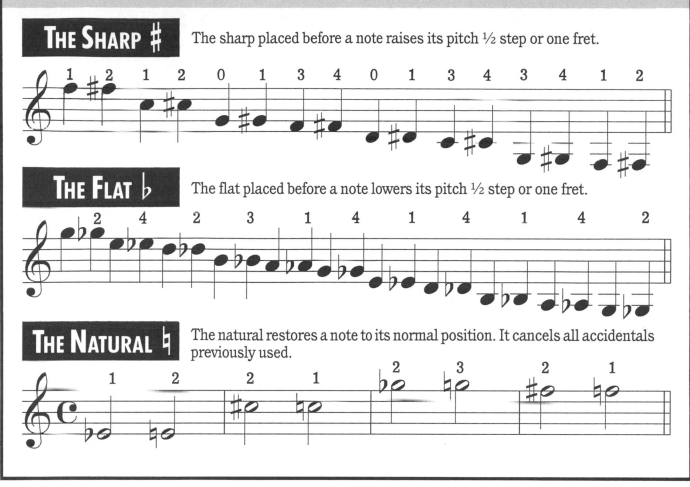

THE FLAT ♭ The flat placed before a note lowers its pitch ½ step or one fret.

THE NATURAL ♮ The natural restores a note to its normal position. It cancels all accidentals previously used.

Running Around

Teacher Acc.

Mel Bay

Home, Home, Can I Forget Thee

Arr. by Mel Bay

Guitar Solo

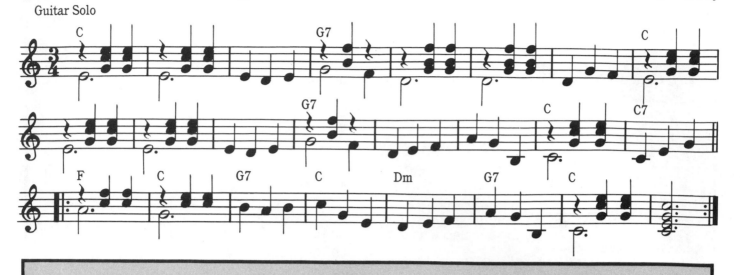

TEMPO

TEMPO is the rate of speed of a musical composition. Three types of tempos used in this book will be:
ANDANTE: A slow, easy pace.　　　MODERATO: Moderate.　　　ALLEGRO: Lively.

Playtime

Pleyel
Arr. by Mel Bay

Guitar Duet
Moderato

Count:　3　　1　2　3

THE KEY OF A MINOR

(Relative to C Major)

Each major key will have a relative minor key.

The relative minor scale is built upon the sixth tone of the major scale.

The key signature of both will be the same.

The minor scale will have the same number of tones (7) as the major.

The difference between the two scales is the arrangement of the whole steps and half steps.

There are three forms of the minor scale: 1) pure or natural, 2) harmonic, 3) melodic.

THE A MINOR SCALE

Natural (Pure)

Harmonic

The 7th tone is raised one half step ascending and descending.

Melodic

The 6th and 7th tones are raised one half step ascending and lowered back to their normal pitch descending.

THE CHORDS IN THE KEY OF A MINOR

M = Minor

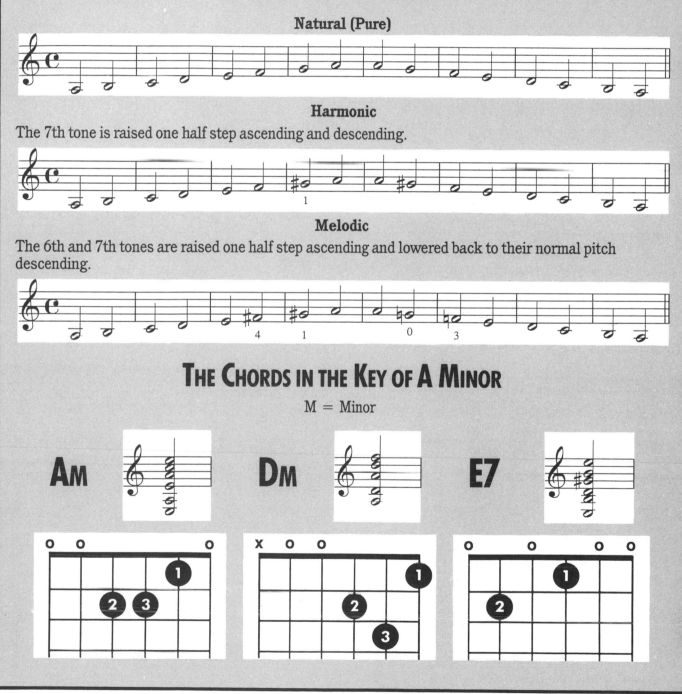

AM   DM   E7

Accompaniment Styles in A Minor

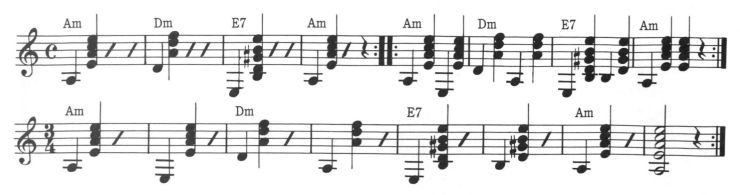

Orchestration Style

The diagonal line (/) indicates a chord stroke. They will fall only on each beat of the measure.

Repeat the accompaniment exercises until they can be played without missing a beat.

A Daily Scale Study in A Minor

Harmonic

(*Repeat* ⊓∨⊓∨)

Hold Sign: ⌒ This sign placed over or under a note or rest indicates the prolonging of its time value.

Wayfarin' Stranger

Slowly
Chord Acc.

FIRST AND SECOND ENDINGS

Sometimes two endings are required in certain selections…one to lead back into a repeated chorus and one to close it. They will be shown like this:

The first time, play the bracketed ending No. 1. Repeat the chorus. The second time, skip the first ending and play ending No. 2.

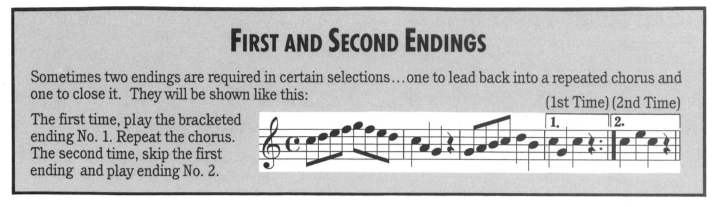

Cradle Song

Johann Brahms

WORDS INDICATING VARIATIONS OF TEMPO

RITARDANDO or RITARD (rit.)…To grow slower   ACCELERANDO (acc.)…To increase the speed

Billy's Duet

*D.C. al Fine…Repeat from the beginning to the word "Fine."

33

Another Daily Scale Study in A Minor

(Repeat ⊓ V ⊓ V)

A Visit to the Relatives

C Major

A Minor (Harmonic)

Melodic

C Major

Careless Love

Song Without Words

Guitar Duet

Arr. by Mel Bay

Terry's Tune

Mel Bay

D.C. al Fine *

*D.C. al Fine means to go back to the beginning and play until the word "Fine" or "End" appears.

THE KEY OF G

The key of G will have one sharp (F♯). It will be identified by this signature:

The F notes will be played as shown:

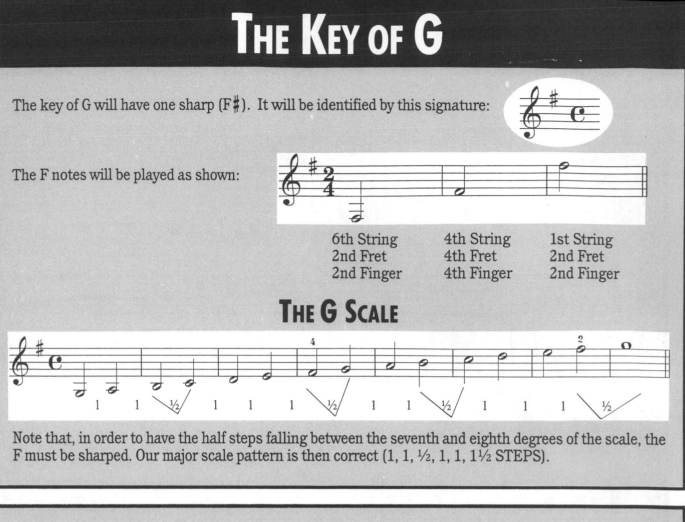

6th String	4th String	1st String
2nd Fret	4th Fret	2nd Fret
2nd Finger	4th Finger	2nd Finger

THE G SCALE

Note that, in order to have the half steps falling between the seventh and eighth degrees of the scale, the F must be sharped. Our major scale pattern is then correct (1, 1, ½, 1, 1, 1½ STEPS).

TWO-FOUR TIME

This sign 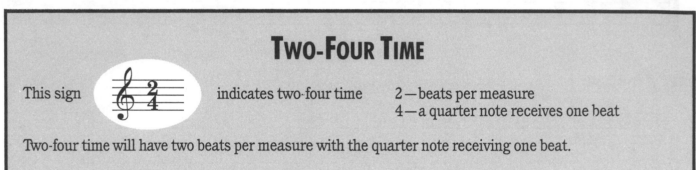 indicates two-four time 2—beats per measure
4—a quarter note receives one beat

Two-four time will have two beats per measure with the quarter note receiving one beat.

In the Evening by the Moonlight

A Daily Drill

CHORDS IN THE KEY OF G

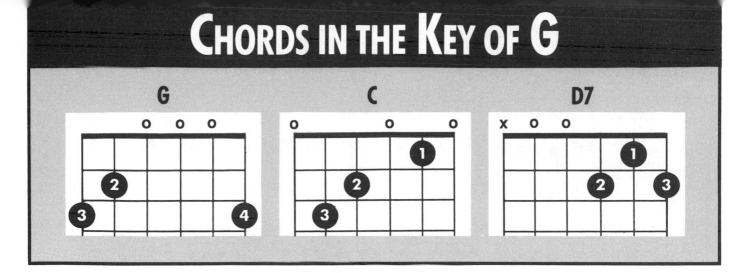

Accompaniment Styles in the Key of G

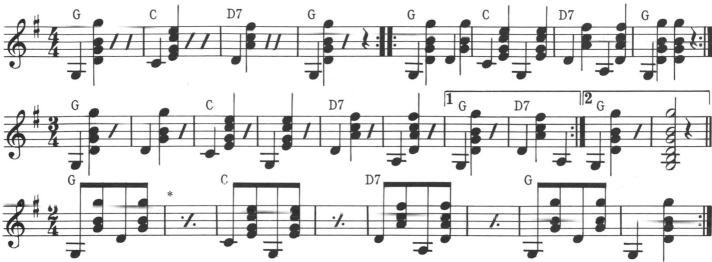

*This sign (%) means that the previous measure is to be repeated.

The following etude introduces the notes D and B being played together. This is done by playing the note D with the first finger on the third fret of the second string and playing the note B with the second finger on the fourth fret of the THIRD STRING.

Etude

The Old Mill

Guitar Duet

Arr. by Mel Bay

Moderato

Fine

D.C. al Fine

A Scale Study

Count:

1 2 & 3 & 4 &

(Repeat ⊓∨)

A Serenade

Guitar Solo

Mel Bay

Moderato

G   D7   D9   D9 D7 G°   G

G7   C   C#°   D7   D9 D7   1. G   D7   2. G

Austrian Hymn

Guitar Duet

Haydn
Arr. by Mel Bay

Andante

Home on the Range

> = Accent

Arr. by Mel Bay

Guitar Solo

Andante

The Little Prince

Guitar Duet

Mazas
Arr. by Mel Bay

Andante

Carry Me Back to Old Virginny

Guitar Solo

Bland
Arr. by Mel Bay

Andante

*The wavy line before the last chord means to glide the pick slowly over the strings, producing a harp-like effect. The musical term for this is QUASI ARPI.

THE KEY OF E MINOR

(Relative to G Major)

The key of E minor will have the same key signature as G major.

TWO E MINOR SCALES

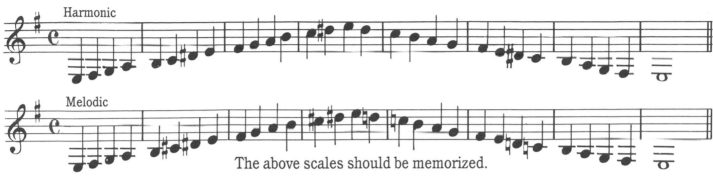

The above scales should be memorized.

THE CHORDS IN THE KEY OF E MINOR

The chords in the key of E minor are:

Em   Am   B7

Accompaniment Styles in the Key of E Minor

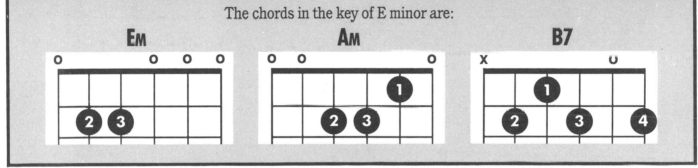

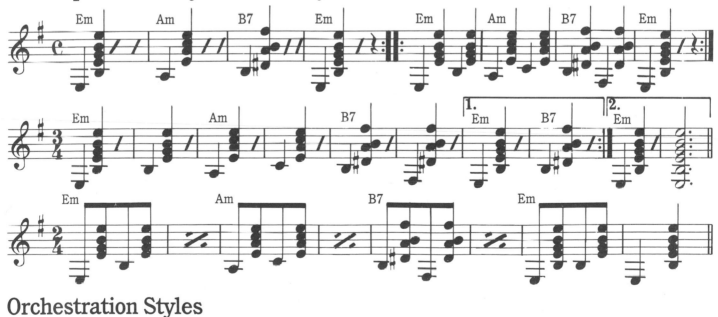

Orchestration Styles

Morning Song

American Folk Hymn

Cindy

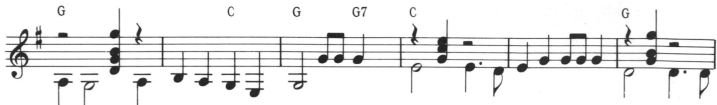

Night Song

Sor
Arr. by Mel Bay

RITARD

42

A CHORD REVIEW

The key of C has six chords. They are C, F, G7, Am, Dm, and E7.
The latter three are in the relative minor key but use the key signature of C.

A7

All "outside" chords are ACCIDENTAL CHORDS.
The most commonly used of these chords are D7 and A7.
The six chords found in the key of G are G, C, D7, Em, Am, and B7.
The most common accidental chords found in the key of G are A7 and E7.

Spotting the accidentals in the various chords will facilitate the reading of them...for example:

B7 will have a D♯

E7 will have a G♯

A7 will have a C♯

D7 will have a F♯

In the following studies, you will see how they appear.

Lament

Guitar Solo

Mel Bay

Maytime

Guitar Duet

TONE

Music is composed of sounds pleasant to the ear.

SOUND may be made from NOISE or TONE.

NOISE is made by irregular vibrations such as would be caused by striking a table with a hammer, the shot of a gun, or slapping two stones together.

TONE is produced by regular vibrations as would be caused by drawing a bow over the strings of a violin, striking the strings of a guitar, or blowing through a wind instrument such as a trumpet.

A tone has four characteristics...PITCH, DURATION, DYNAMICS, and TIMBRE.

PITCH: the highness or lowness of a tone.

DURATION: the length of a tone.

DYNAMICS: the force or power of a tone (loudness or softness).

TIMBRE: quality of the tone.

A note represents the pitch and duration of a tone.

Dynamics are indicated by words such as...

Pianissimo	(*pp*)	very soft
Piano	(*p*)	soft
Mezzo piano	(*mp*)	medium soft
Mezzo forte	(*mf*)	medium loud
Forte	(*f*)	very loud

Timbre depends upon the skill of the performer plus the quality of the instrument which is being played.

Rondo

Guitar Duet

Mazas, Op. 85
Arr. by Mel Bay

Allegro

Student should
play both parts

Count: 1 & 2 &   1- 2   1 & 2 &   1   2   1 & 2 &

Sor's Waltz

Arr. by Mel Bay

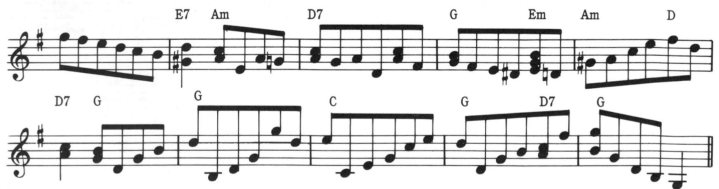

Bluegrass Waltz

Mel Bay

Running the Thirds in G

A Little Bit of Hanon

Mel Bay

Southern Fried

Mel Bay

Certificate of Completion

This is to certify that

_____

Student's Name

has now completed *Mel Bay's Modern Guitar Method Grade 1* and is now ready to enter *Mel Bay's Modern Guitar Method Grade 2*.

_____

Teacher's Name

_____

Date